BOB DYLAN
SHADOWS IN THE NIGHT

WISE PUBLICATIONS
PART OF THE MUSIC SALES GROUP

LONDON / NEW YORK / PARIS / SYDNEY / COPENHAGEN / BERLIN / MADRID / HONG KONG / TOKYO

PUBLISHED BY
WISE PUBLICATIONS
14-15 BERNERS STREET, LONDON W1T 3LJ, UK.

EXCLUSIVE DISTRIBUTORS:
MUSIC SALES LIMITED
DISTRIBUTION CENTRE, NEWMARKET ROAD,
BURY ST EDMUNDS, SUFFOLK IP33 3YB, UK.

MUSIC SALES CORPORATION
180 MADISON AVENUE, 24TH FLOOR,
NEW YORK NY 10016, USA.

MUSIC SALES PTY LIMITED
4TH FLOOR, LISGAR HOUSE, 30-32 CARRINGTON STREET,
SYDNEY, NSW 2000, AUSTRALIA.

ORDER NO. AM1010834
ISBN: 978-1-78558-010-9
THIS BOOK © COPYRIGHT 2015 WISE PUBLICATIONS,
A DIVISION OF MUSIC SALES LIMITED.

EDITED BY JENNI NOREY.
MUSIC ARRANGED BY VASCO HEXEL.
MUSIC PROCESSED BY PAUL EWERS MUSIC DESIGN.
PHOTOGRAPHY BY JOHN SHEARER.
DESIGN BY GEOFF GANS.

PRINTED IN THE EU.

I'm a Fool to Want You

Words & Music by Frank Sinatra, Jack Wolf & Joel Herron

kiss that the dev-il has known.___

Time_____ and time a-gain   I said I'd

leave you.___

Time_____ and time a-gain   I____ went a-

-way.

But then would come a time   when_ I would

need you   and once   a-gain   are these words   I {had / have} to

THE NIGHT WE CALLED IT A DAY

Words by Tom Adair
Music by Matt Dennis

Stay With Me

Words & Music by Carolyn Leigh & Jerome Moross

stum-ble__ on the way, stay with me.__ Like the lamb that in spring-time wan-ders far from the fold, comes the dark-ness and the frost, I get lost,

I grow cold. I grow cold, I grow wea-ry,__ and I know I have sinned, and I go seek-ing shel-ter and I cry in the

wind. Though I grope and I blun-der and I'm weak and I'm wrong, though the

road buck-les un-der where I walk, walk a-long. Till I find to my

won-der ev-'ry path leads to thee, all that I can do is pray, stay with

me. Stay with me.

Autumn Leaves

Words by Jacques Prevert
Music by Joseph Kosma

The fall - ing leaves drift by the win - dow,

Why Try to Change Me Now

Words by Joseph McCarthy
Music by Cy Coleman

I'm sen-ti-men-tal,__ so I walk in the rain.

I've got some ha-bits__ e-ven I can't ex-plain. Could start for the cor-ner,

turn up in Spain. Why try to change me now?___

I sit and day-dream,___ I've got day-dreams ga-lore.___ Ci - ga-rette ash- es, there they

go on the floor, I'll go a-way week - ends, leave my keys___ in the door,___

but why try to change me now?___ Why can't I be more___

I was al - ways your clown? Why try to change me now?___

Don't you re-mem-ber I was al - ways___ your clown? But why try to change me,___

why try to change me___ now?_____

Some Enchanted Evening

Words by Oscar Hammerstein II
Music by Richard Rodgers

night, as strange as it seems, the sound of___ her

laugh-ter___ will sing___ in your dreams.

Who can ex-plain it, who can tell you why? Fools give you rea-sons, wise men nev-er try.

Some en-chan-ted eve - ning, when you find your true love,

Full Moon and Empty Arms

Words by Buddy Kaye & Ted Mossman
Music by Buddy Kaye, Ted Mossman
& Sergei Rachmaninoff

Full moon and___ emp-ty arms,___ the moon is there for us to share. But where are you? A night like

this could weave a mem - o - ry and ev - 'ry

poco rit.

kiss could start a dream for two.____

% **a tempo**

Full moon and____ emp - ty arms,____ to- night, I'll

use the ma - gic moon to wish up - on.

27

And next full moon, if my one wish comes

true, my emp - ty arms will___ be filled with you.

you.

THAT LUCKY OLD SUN

Words by Haven Gillespie
Music by Beasley Smith

WHERE ARE YOU?

Words by Harold Adamson
Music by Jimmy McHugh

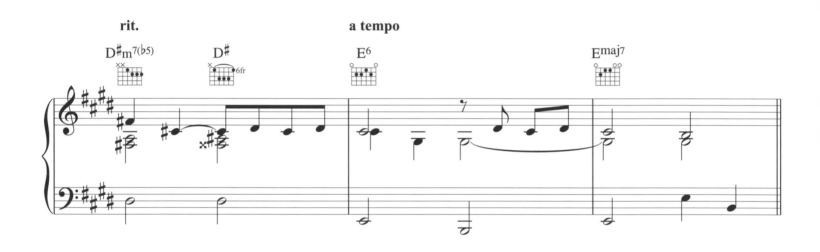

Where are you? Where have you gone with-out me?

When I gave you my love,__ was it all in vain?

All__ life through must I go on pre-tend-ing,

where is my hap-py end-ing? Where are you?

When we said good-bye, love,__ what had we to gain?

What'll I Do

Words & Music by Irving Berlin

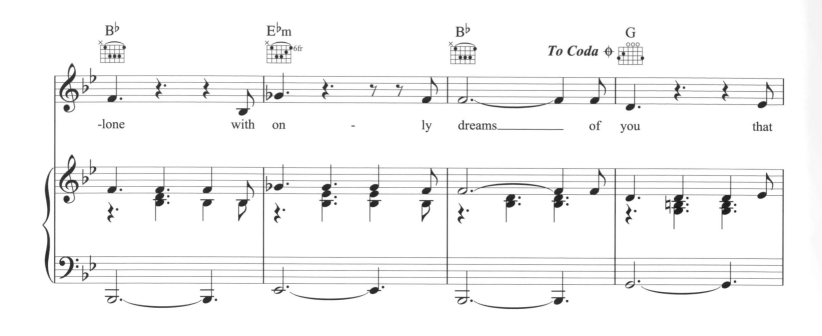

-lone with on - ly dreams_____ of you that

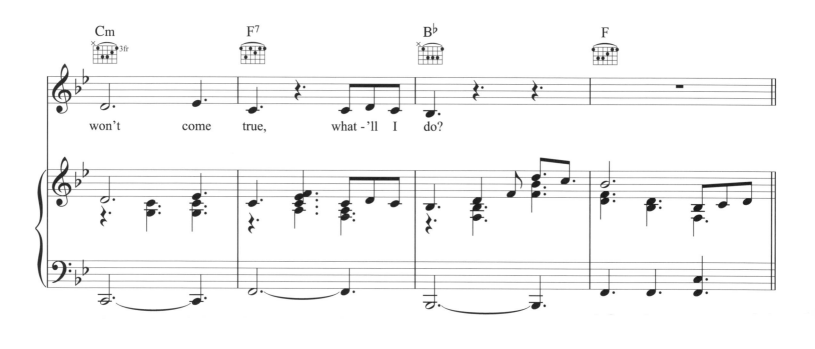

won't come true, what -'ll I do?

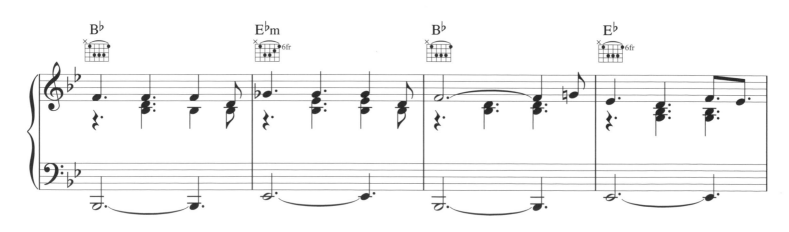

D.S. al Coda

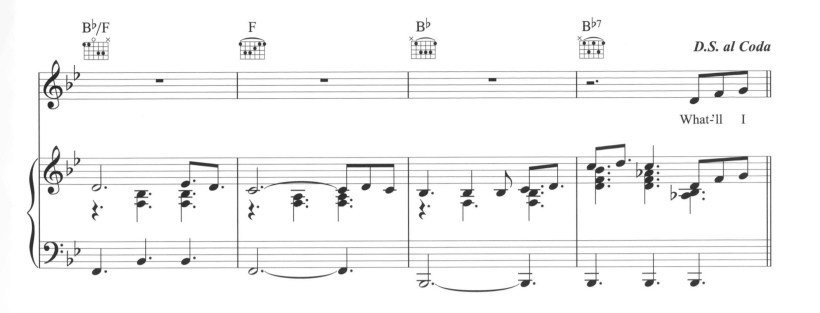

What-'ll I

Coda

you that won't come true, what-'ll I

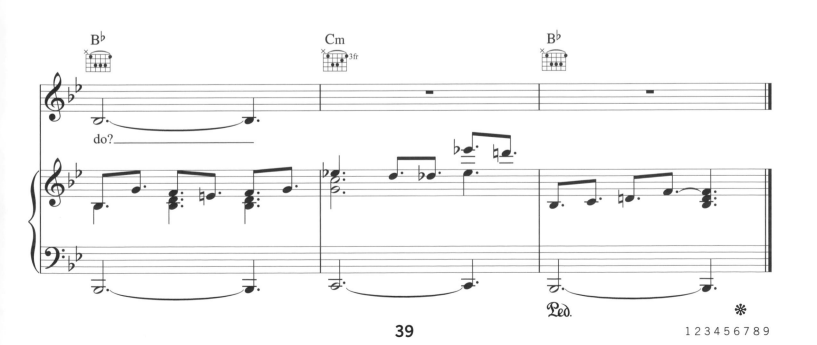

do?

1 2 3 4 5 6 7 8 9

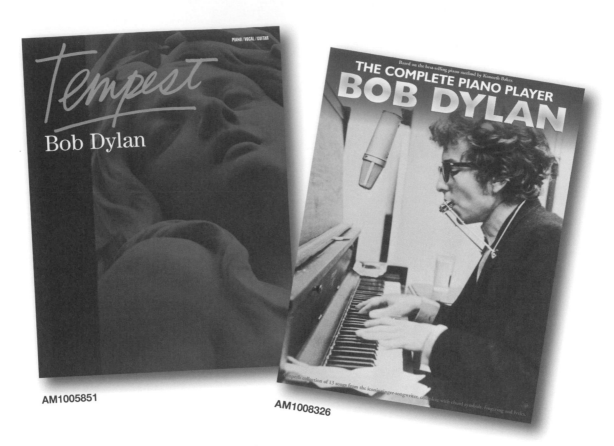

AM1005851

AM1008326

you may also enjoy these other great titles.

AM999339

AM1004641

Available from all good music retailers.

In case of difficulty please contact:
Music Sales Limited, Newmarket Road, Bury St Edmunds, Suffolk, IP33 3YB, UK.
www.musicsales.com